To Peter
with lots of love
for a merry Christmas

Peter

ISBN 0 905652 04 5

Printed and bound by
Morrison & Gibb Ltd, London and Edinburgh

Contents

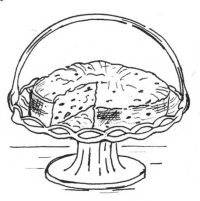

Acknowledgements

I would like to thank Joan Marshall for the cover design of bees working hellebores and Lily Studt and David Smith for the illustrations.

J. White.
Denham, Suffolk, 1978.

Introduction

HONEY is a unique substance—a food produced by flowers and collected from them and stored by honeybees. It is estimated that to collect a pound of honey bees must fly a distance equivalent to two to three orbits of the earth, and will visit up to a million flowers to do so.

HONEY is a mixture of sugars which are inverted by enzymes produced by the bees. This means that it is readily assimilated by our digestive system, and is a source of immediately available nourishment.

From earliest times honey has been known to man as a food and as an ingredient of medicine. Crucibles of honey have been found in ancient Egyptian tombs and we read in the Old Testament that Jacob sent Benjamin into Egypt with gifts of 'the best fruits of the land—balm, honey, spices and myrrh, nuts and almonds'.

The *COLOUR OF HONEY* which can vary from almost water white to a dark brown, the *FLAVOUR* and the *AROMA* are dependant on the flowers from which it was gathered. Honey from Rosebay Willowherb and Clover is quite light in colour, that from Hawthorn is deep amber. Heather is a deep golden brown while Sycamore is very dark.

HONEY will crystallise after it has been extracted, some kinds more quickly than others, but if gently warmed it will soon become liquid again.

HONEY should be stored in a cool dry place and should always be covered with a tightly fitting lid. Even when on the table the lid should be replaced after serving to preserve the delicate aroma. There are many ways of using honey but care must be taken that it is not overheated so that the flavour is spoiled, nor that the flavour and aroma are masked by other strongly flavoured ingredients.

Although honey could be substituted for sugar in many recipes, it is an expensive commodity, and it is thus only economical to use it in small quantities and when its flavour improves the dish.

Oven Temperatures

This compares oven thermostats marked in °C with those marked in °F and gas marks. They are not exact conversions but are based on dial markings.

Oven Heat	°C	°F	Gas mark
very cool	110	225	$\frac{1}{4}$
	120	250	$\frac{1}{2}$
cool	140	275	1
slow	150	300	2
moderately slow	160–170	325	3
moderate	180	350	4
moderately hot	190	375	5
hot	200	400	6
very hot	220	425	7
,, ,,	230	450	8
,, ,,	240	475	9
	260	500	
	270	525	

Average Composition of Honey

100g Honey contains the following:

Water	17.2 g
Fructose	38.2 g
Glucose	31.3 g
Sucrose	1.3 g
Other sugars	8.8 g
Potassium	10 mg
Sodium	5 mg
Calcium	5 mg
Magnesium	6 mg
Iron	0.5 mg
Copper	0.2 mg
Manganese	0.2 mg
Phosphate	16.0 mg
Sulphate	5.0 mg

Trace amounts of nicotinic acid, pantothenic acid, pyridoxin, riboflavin, thiamin, biotin, folic acid, ascorbic acid, several enzymes, traces of lipids and many other substances.

To use honey in cooking.—Honey is easier to measure in a spoon if the spoon is warmed.
To weigh honey.—Place the jar on the scales and take out honey until the weight is reduced by the required amount.

Metric quantities are given first with imperial in brackets. Use one or the other as the amounts are not exactly the same.

Breakfast

PORRIDGE

Porridge is still regarded by many as the best start to the day.
Make it in your usual way and stir in as much honey as you
want when it is on the plate. Heather honey is particularly
good with porridge, and if stone ground oats are used the result
is a nourishing meal.

For those who prefer an instant breakfast such as cornflakes,
Shredded Wheat, Weetabix, or bran etc, try a spoonful of
honey on them before adding the milk.

GRAPEFRUIT

This is better if prepared overnight.

Cut a grapefruit in half, loosen the segments and cut out the
pips and core from the centre.

Put 1 or 2 × 5 ml (tsp) spoons of honey on top and leave
overnight. By morning the honey and fruitjuice will have
blended together.

YOGURT

Home made yogurt is delicious sweetened with honey, or with
honey and fresh fruit added.

Honey with Salads

When the conventional salad ingredients are expensive and difficult to obtain in winter try this:

WINTER ORANGE SALAD
1 small or ½ large white cabbage
1 orange
1 cooking apple
10 ml (2 tsp) lemon juice
5 ml (1 tsp) honey
10 ml (2 tsp) wine vinegar or dry wine
30 ml (1½ tbs) olive oil
seasoning

Slice the cabbage and apple thinly, cut the orange into small pieces and mix together. Beat the rest of the ingredients together until smooth to make a dressing. Season to taste. Either pour the sauce over the salad or serve separately.
    If preferred a salad dressing can be made without oil.

HONEY AND CIDER VINEGAR DRESSING
5 ml (1 tsp) honey
½ cup cider vinegar
salt and pepper to taste

Mix all ingredients together, stirring well.

6

NORTH SEA SAUCE—a salad dressing

1 small tin of evaporated milk
1½ tins wine or cider vinegar (measured in the milk tin)
20 ml (1 tbs) honey
salt, pepper and mustard powder to taste

Whisk all ingredients together and add seasoning as required.
This will keep well but may need occasional shaking.

A WINTER SALAD—Cole Slaw type

¼ of a white cabbage or 4 brussels sprouts finely shredded
  (Brussels sprouts give a more 'nutty' flavour)
1 carrot, finely grated
1 small onion or 1 leek, finely sliced
1 apple, grated
a little chopped green pepper, if available
40 ml (2 tbs) mayonnaise
20 ml (1 tbs) honey
20 ml (1 tbs) cider vinegar or wine vinegar

Blend the mayonnaise, honey and vinegar well, then mix with
the chopped or sliced vegetables.
    Serve with cheese or cold meats.

MAYONNAISE

1 egg
5 ml (1 tsp) honey
100 ml (4 fl. oz) cider or wine vinegar
300 ml (12 fl. oz) corn oil
salt and pepper

Blend the egg, seasoning and honey, adding the oil in small
amounts (a hand mixer is ideal) until smooth and thick. Stir in
the vinegar.

7

VINAIGRETTE SAUCE

40 ml (2 tbs) corn or sunflower oil
25 ml (4 tsp) wine vinegar
5 ml (1 tsp) honey
sea salt
freshly ground pepper

Mix all ingredients together and season to taste. Use a blender or shake vigorously in a screw topped jar.

AVOCADO PEARS

The conventional way to serve these is with mayonnaise or French dressing, but if you would like a change try this way:
    Halve the pear lengthwise and remove the stone.
    Fill the cavity with loganberries or raspberries and pour a spoonful of honey over the fruit.
    Serve cold.

GLOBE ARTICHOKES

Trim the stalks and any hard outside leaves.
    Drop the artichokes, tops downward into boiling, lightly salted water and simmer for about 20 mins. or until the leaves pull out easily. Serve hot, dipping the leaves into any of the following:

    Melted butter or margarine blended with honey.
    Warmed honey.
    Vinaigrette sauce.

8

Honey with Fruit

FRESH FRUIT SALAD

Fresh fruit salad can be enjoyed all through the year and can be made from most fruits. No two need ever be the same and almost any combination of fruits can be used.

Some melon is a good base as it provides plenty of juice, but if drier fruits are the only ones available, use fruit squash or add a little water to the honey to make a syrup.

The following fruits are suitable: bananas, melon, apples, pears, sweet plums, cherries, currants, strawberries, fresh pineapple, loganberries, raspberries, blackberries, oranges, grapes and peaches.

Tinned pineapple could provide a syrup and a contrasting flavour in some cases.

Try and make your salad interesting in colour, a few frozen raspberries will make a great difference to the appearance of a winter salad which is mostly apple, banana and orange. Prepare all fruit by cutting it into small pieces and removing stones, pips and pith. It is advisable to cut bananas first and put them in the bottom of the dish as they quickly discolour. When all the fruit is in the bowl, pour a little honey over it, the amount will vary according to the sweetness of the fruit. Cover with a lid or film and stir occasionally to blend the fruit with the juices.

Serve cold with cream, ice cream, junket, jelly, yogurt etc.

9

FRUIT SALAD

This recipe for fruit salad will make 50 servings for a party.

½ kilo (1 lb) grapes
½ kilo (1 lb) apples
1 kilo (2 lb) dessert pears
1 kilo (2 lb) soft fruit in season, raspberries strawberries
  loganberries etc.
12 bananas
1 tin or 4 fresh mandarin oranges
1 tin cherries (or fresh if available)
1 tin peaches (or 4 fresh peaches)
1 melon
500 g (1 lb) honey

Open the tinned fruit and put into a large bowl. Remove the
seeds from the grapes and cut in halves. Remove seeds and
peel from the melon and cut into small squares. Add the
bananas sliced finely, the peaches cut in thin slices, the apples
grated and the oranges cut up after removing pips and pith.
When all the fruit is in the bowl pour the liquid honey over
and stir in. Cover and leave in a cool place, stirring at intervals.
If it appears to need more liquid add tinned or bottled orange
juice.

FRUIT SYRUP

This syrup will make a very palatable base for a fresh fruit
salad for a special occasion.

50 g (2 oz) honey
finely grated rind and juice of a lemon
40 ml (2 tbs) orange juice
40 ml (2 tbs) dry sherry

Put the ingredients in a bowl and stand in a warm place until
they will blend together. Strain and chill, then add to the fruit.

10

MELON

Remove the pips and cut the melon into wedges or cubes and place on serving plates.

Pour 1 or 2–5 ml (tsp) spoons of honey over each wedge or dish of cubes. Leave for an hour for the melon juice and honey to blend together. Sprinkle with chopped crystallised ginger or powdered ginger to individual taste.

BAKED APPLES

Well baked apples are a favourite with most people and are delicious served with cream or yogurt.

Bramley apples are a good variety for baking.

Wash the apples and remove the cores.

Place the plug from the botton under each apple on a baking dish. Fill the centre hole with either dates, raisins, blackberries etc.

Pour 2 × 5 ml (tsp) spoons of honey on to the centre filling of each apple.

Put a little water in the dish (about 0.5 cm) and bake at 275–325° F for 1½ hours or until soft. Baste occasionally.

Serve with cream, custard or yogurt.

APPLE AND NUT DESSERT

4 dessert apples
juice of 2 oranges (or equivalent in bottled orange juice)
50–100 g (2–4 oz) walnuts or hazelnuts
honey to taste
cream, yogurt or custard

Wash the apples, grate into a bowl and cover with orange juice.

Chop or mill the nuts and add to the apple mixture.

Sweeten with honey to taste and mix well.

Put into serving glasses and decorate with cream, custard or yogurt.

APPLE WHIP

450 g (1 lb) cooking apples
150 ml (6 fl. oz) water
a few cloves
1 small can evaporated milk
50 g (2 oz) honey
20 ml (1 tbs) lemon juice

Peel, core and cut up the apples, put them in a pan with the cloves and water and simmer gently until soft. Remove cloves and either sieve, mash, or liquidise apples.

Beat the evaporated milk until it doubles in size, fold in the honey, apple and lemon juice.

Divide into four glasses and decorate with whipped cream, yogurt, angelica or nuts.

Note: If evaporated milk is treated in the following way it will be much easier to whip.

Place the can of milk, unopened in a saucepan of water and bring the water to the boil, simmer it for about 5 minutes.

Pour off the water and cool the milk either under the cold water tap or standing in a bowl of ice. Leave in the refrigerator until required. Add a few drops of lemon juice before whipping.

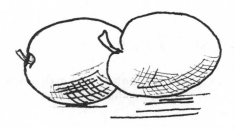

APPLE AND RAISIN MERINGUE

450 g (1 lb) cooking apples
100 g (4 oz) raisins
50 g (2 oz) honey
the juice of an orange or 40 ml (2 tbs) bottled orange juice
2 egg whites
50 g (2 oz) castor sugar

Slice the apples and put them with the raisins and orange
juice in a covered pan. Cook very gently either on top of the
stove or in the oven until the apples are soft. Mix in the honey
and pour into a dish.

Whisk the egg whites until stiff, then whisk in half the
sugar. Stir in the rest of the sugar and spoon this meringue
over the top of the apple mixture. Put in a slow oven,
275–300° F for about 20 mins. to half an hour, until the
meringue is light golden and crisp. Serve hot or cold.

APPLE AND LEMON MERINGUE

Follow the above recipe using 5 ml (1 tsp) grated lemon rind
instead of raisins.

LEMON SNOW

Rind and juice of 1½ lemons
40 g (1½ oz) honey
250 ml (½ pint) water
15 g (½ oz) gelatine
1 egg white

Dissolve the gelatine in a little of the water in a warm place.

Thinly peel the lemon rind, putting it in a small pan with the
rest of the water and bring to the boil. Strain onto the gelatine,
and stir well until dissolved, then stir in the honey.

Allow to cool, then chill until just beginning to set.

Add the lemon juice and egg white and whisk until frothy.

Pile into a dish and leave to set.

BANANA CUSTARD

250 ml (½ pint) milk
2 eggs
25 g (1 oz) sugar

} or 250 ml (½ pint) custard made with custard powder

4 bananas
50 g (2 oz) dates
20 ml honey (1 tbs)
chopped walnuts to garnish

Peel and slice the bananas and chop the dates. Put them in a dish and pour the honey over them, mix well.

Slowly cook the milk, beaten eggs and sugar over low heat, stirring well until it thickens, or make up custard from custard powder.

Divide the fruit mixture into four serving dishes, pour the custard over the top and allow to cool.

Sprinkle chopped walnuts over the top or decorate with whipped cream.

Honey Puddings and Sweets

Steamed puddings are delicious when honey is used as an ingredient, for they are cooked at a sufficiently low temperature not to spoil the flavour of the honey, and when cooked have an attractive golden colour.

Honey is best suited to those puddings with a light flavour, where its own delicate flavour is not masked.

DATE PUDDING
100 g (4 oz) dates
50 g (2 oz) flour ⎫
50 g (2 oz) breadcrumbs ⎬ or 100 g (4 oz) flour
75 g (3 oz) honey
75 g (3 oz) suet or margarine
2.5 ml (½ tsp) baking powder
1 egg
a little milk

Put all the dry ingredients into a bowl. Rub in the fat. Whisk the egg until it is light in colour, then whisk in the honey. Add to the dry ingredients using a little milk to make it a soft dropping consistency. Pour into a greased basin and cover with a lid or greased paper tied down. Steam for 2–2½ hours.

Turn out and serve very hot with a syrup made from lemon or orange juice and honey.

STEAMED ORANGE PUDDING

100 g (4 oz) butter or margarine
100 g (4 oz) honey
2 eggs
the grated rind of an orange
125 g (5 oz) self-raising flour
a little milk if required

Cream the margarine and honey and beat in the eggs. Add the grated orange rind. Fold in the flour and if required add a little milk to make it a soft consistency. Grease a basin, pour in the mixture, cover with a lid or greased paper and steam for 1½ to 2 hours.

Turn out of the basin and serve hot with an orange sauce.

WHOLE LEMON PUDDING

Pastry
200 g (8 oz) self-raising flour
100 g (4 oz) suet or margarine
salt—a pinch
water

Sift flour and salt into a basin, rub in the fat and add sufficient cold water to make a soft dough. Roll out and use two-thirds of it to line a 1 litre (2 pint) basin.

Filling
200 g (8 oz) honey (or 100 g (4 oz) honey and
      50 g (2 oz) sugar)
1 large ripe lemon
100 g (4 oz) breadcrumbs

Mix honey and breadcrumbs, and fill the pastry in the basin placing the whole lemon in the centre of the pudding.

Cover with a lid of the remaining pastry and seal the edges well.

Cover with greased paper, then foil or a cloth. Tie down and steam for 3 to 4 hours, when the lemon should feel soft when tested with a skewer. Serve hot.

WHOLE ORANGE PUDDING

As above but using a thin skinned orange instead of a lemon, and 50 g (4 oz) honey.

QUEEN OF PUDDINGS

250 ml (½ pint) milk
25 g (1 oz) butter or margarine
50 g (2 oz) breadcrumbs
the grated rind of an orange or a lemon
    or a few drops of vanilla essence
20 ml (1 tbs) honey
2 small egg yolks or 1 large
raspberry or other red jam

Meringue
1 or 2 egg whites
50 g (2 oz) castor sugar

Place the milk and butter in a pan and warm.
    Pour over the breadcrumbs and leave to soak for at least 10 mins.
    Stir in the grated rind, egg yolks and honey and mix well.
    Pour into a greased pie dish.
    Bake in a moderate oven 350–375° F until set. Remove from the oven and reduce the heat to 300° F.
    Coat the top of the pudding with raspberry jam.
    Whisk the egg whites until stiff, lightly fold in the sugar and pile on top of the pudding.
    Put a dusting of castor sugar over the top and return to the oven until the meringue is brown and crisp.

    For a different flavour leave out the lemon rind and moisten the breadcrumbs with sherry or mead.

Upside Down Puddings and Cakes

This is an idea we have copied from the Americans and the dish looks attractive when brought to the table. There are many variations according to the fruit available. Here are a few suggestions:

APPLE AND GINGER UPSIDE DOWN PUDDING

Apple topping
50 g (2 oz) margarine or butter
50 g (2 oz) honey
a little ground cinnamon or apple pie spice
3 medium or 2 large cooking apples

Gingerbread
150 g (6 oz) flour
2.5 ml ($\frac{1}{2}$ tsp) baking powder
2.5 ml ($\frac{1}{2}$ tsp) ground ginger
25 g (1 oz) soft brown sugar
20 ml (1 tbs) golden syrup or honey
35 g ($1\frac{1}{2}$ oz) butter or margarine
125 ml ($\frac{1}{4}$ pint) sour milk
1 egg

Topping
Melt the margarine and honey and put in the bottom of a 17.5 cm (7 in.) square tin. Chop the apples finely and sprinkle with the spice. Pack them on top of the margarine and honey and press down firmly.

18

Pudding

Put the dry ingredients in a bowl, put the milk, syrup and treacle in a pan to warm. Beat the egg. Rub the fat into the dry ingredients, add the syrup and egg and mix together to a heavy pouring consistency. Pour over the apple and cook at 350° F for about 40 mins. Allow to cool a little before turning out onto a dish, then serve with cream, yogurt, custard or plain.

PINEAPPLE UPSIDE DOWN CAKE

Topping
slices of pineapple
cherries
50 g (2 oz) margarine or butter
50 g (2 oz) honey

Cake mixture
75 g (3 oz) margarine or butter
75 g (3 oz) castor sugar
75 (3 oz) self-raising flour
2 small or 1 large egg

Melt the margarine in the bottom of a 20 cm (8 in.) round tin and stir in the honey. Arrange the fruit decoratively in this mixture.

Grease the sides of the tin.

Cream the sugar and margarine until light and fluffy, add the eggs, then fold in the flour. Spread over the fruit and bake at 375–400° F for 30–35 mins.

Allow to shrink a little in the tin before turning out.

Serve warm with cream, or with a sauce made from the fruit juice and cornflour.

This cake could also be served cold for tea.

Alternative suggestions of fruit for this recipe:
Apple with blackberries.
Pears with cherries or prunes (stew the prunes first).
Raspberries and redcurrants arranged in circles.
Apricots and chopped walnuts.

19

BREAD AND BUTTER PUDDING

2–3 slices of bread and butter
40 g (1½ oz) honey
50 g. (2 oz) sultanas
25 g (1 oz) chopped candied peel
400 ml (¾ pint) milk
2 eggs
a little grated nutmeg

Grease a pie dish well. Spread the bread and butter with the honey.

Cut the bread into small squares and place in layers in the dish with the sultanas and peel, the last layer to be bread and butter.

Warm the milk and add it to the beaten eggs, mix well, then pour over the bread and butter in the pie dish and leave to soak for half an hour.

Grate a little nutmeg on the top.

Bake at 375° F for about 45 mins. until the custard is set and the top is golden brown and crisp.

Serve hot.

BREAD AND BUTTER PUDDING WITH MARIGOLD PETALS

2 to 3 slices bread and butter
40 g (1½ oz) honey
400 ml (¾ pint) milk
2 eggs
1 heaped 20 ml (1 tbs) spoonful of marigold (calendula) petals

Follow the previous recipe, using the petals instead of fruit.

HONEYCOMB CREAMS

3 small or 2 large eggs
35 g (1½ oz) honey
500 ml (1 pint) milk
vanilla essence
15 g (½ oz) gelatine
20 ml (1 tbs) water
glace cherries, flaked almonds or chocolate shreds
   for decoration

Separate the eggs and beat the yolks. Put the milk and honey
in a pan to warm. When hot (not boiling), pour it over the
eggs. Return to the pan and stir constantly over low heat using
a wooden spoon until it thickens and will coat the back of the
spoon.

Remove from the heat, add the flavouring and pour into a
bowl to cool.

Dissolve the gelatine in warm water and add to the custard,
stirring it in well. When nearly set whisk it slightly.

Clean and dry the whisk, then whisk the egg whites until
they are stiff, then fold them gently into the custard with a
metal spoon.

Pour into glasses to set.

Decorate with cherries, nuts chocolate etc. and serve cold.

HONEY LEMON CREAM PIE

the finely grated rind and juice of 1 large lemon
50 g (2 oz) margarine or butter
100 g (4 oz) digestive biscuits, crushed finely
25 g (1 oz) soft brown sugar
20 ml (1 tbs) honey
a small can of evaporated milk (previously brought
   to the boil in a pan of water then chilled)
40 ml (2 tbs) water
15 g (½ oz) gelatine

Melt the fat in a pan, remove from the heat and stir in the
biscuit crumbs and brown sugar.

Press into a 17.5 cm (7 in.) cake tin with a loose bottom and put in a refrigerator to set for about half an hour.

Whisk the evaporated milk and lemon juice until thick.

Add the grated rind and honey and whisk in.

Put the water in a basin, stir in the gelatine and stand in a warm place stirring until dissolved. Add this to the milk and whisk in.

Pour this mixture onto the biscuit crust, put in a refrigerator to set. When set remove from tin and serve cold. It can be decorated with nuts or chocolate shreds.

GROUND RICE CREAM

50 g (2 oz) ground rice
500 ml (1 pint) milk
25 g (1 oz) butter or margarine
20 to 30 ml (1–2 tbs) honey (according to taste)
vanilla flavouring
pink colouring
about 50 ml (2–3 tbs) raspberry jam
decoration—whipped cream, yogurt, coconut,
    chopped nuts etc.

Blend the ground rice with a little of the milk and put the rest of the milk in a saucepan to heat. When it is hot pour it on the ground rice and stir well in.

Return to the heat and cook for about 10 mins. over gentle heat until the rice is thoroughly cooked.

Remove from the heat and stir in the butter, honey, a few drops of vanilla essence and the pink colouring.

Spread the raspberry jam evenly over the bottom of a glass dish and pour the rice mixture over it. Leave it to cool.

Decorate and serve cold.

When serving fruit with a strong flavour such as loganberries or blackberries a milk pudding with a delicate flavour is the best accompaniment.

CORNFLOUR MOULD

500 ml (1 pint) milk
40 g (1½ oz) cornflour
20 ml (1 tbs) honey
25 g (1 oz) margarine or butter
a few drops of vanilla or almond essence

Put the cornflour in a basin with about a quarter of the milk
and blend well. Heat the rest of the milk in a saucepan. Add
the milk to the cornflour in the basin and mix thoroughly.
Return to the pan and bring gently to the boil. Simmer slowly
for about 5 mins. until the cornflour is well cooked.
  Remove from the stove and beat in the butter, honey and
flavouring.
  Pour either into a mould which has been rinsed in cold water
or into individual moulds. Cover to prevent a skin forming.
  Serve with fresh or stewed fruit.

JUNKET

Junket combines the advantages of honey with milk in its most
digestible form, as the rennet enzyme breaks up the curd of
raw milk. As the milk is not boiled all the vitamins are retained
unimpaired.

250 ml (½ pint) milk
25 ml (½ tsp) rennet
10 ml (1 dessertsp) honey
a little grated nutmeg

Warm 250 ml (½ pint) of milk with the honey to 100–105° F
(just above blood heat).
  Remove from the stove and stir in 2.5 ml (½ tsp) rennet,
continue stirring for about half a minute.
  Pour into serving dishes and stand in a warm place to set.
(This should take about half an hour.)
  Sprinkle a little grated nutmeg on top.
  When set it can be put into a refrigerator until required.

Sauces

Honey can be used to sweeten sauces and will add an attractive aroma to them as well as giving a good flavour. The honey is best added after the sauce is cooked.

EGG CUSTARD SAUCE
250 ml (½ pint) milk
a piece of lemon rind (optional)
1 egg or 2 yolks
20 ml (1 tbs) honey

Beat the egg or yolks in a basin. Heat the milk with the piece of rind but do not let it boil.

Pour the milk onto the eggs and stir well.

Return the mixture to the pan. Stand this pan in a larger vessel containing water and cook over the water until the sauce thickens and coats the back of the stirring spoon.

Remove from the heat and stir in the honey, then pour into a dish or sauceboat.

This sauce can be served either hot or cold.

ORANGE SAUCE

1 large orange
20 ml (1 tbs) honey
25 g (1 oz) margarine or butter
15 g (½ oz) cornflour
250 ml (½ pint) water
1 egg yolk (if you do not want to use an egg, omit it and
    add another 5 ml (1 tsp) cornflour)

Wash the orange and squeeze out the juice.

Melt the butter in a saucepan, add the cornflour and cook
for a minute. Add the water gradually and stir well in. Heat
until boiling and simmer for 3 minutes.

Stir in the orange juice and grated rind. Remove from the
heat and stir in the honey and egg yolk (if used).

Pour into a sauceboat and serve either hot or cold.

LEMON SAUCE

Make as for orange sauce using a lemon instead of an orange.

BANANA ICE CREAM

This quantity will make 8 servings.

4 large bananas
225 g (8 oz) honey
100 ml (4 fl. oz) pineapple juice
the juice of a lemon
40 ml (2 tbs) rum (optional)
250 ml (½ pint) cream

Put all the ingredients except the cream into a basin and mix
well. Whip the cream and fold into the mixture.

Place in a refrigerator tray and put in the freezing section
until the edges begin to freeze.

Turn back into the mixing bowl and beat until it is frothy.

Return to the refrigerator tray and freeze until it is set.

Serve in cold glasses.

HONEY SNOW

2 medium sized eggs
60 ml (3 tbs) honey
50 g (2 oz) marshmallows
25 g (1 oz) cornflour
250 ml (½ pint) milk
20 ml (1 tbs) orange squash or juice
20 ml (1 tbs) lemon juice
small bar of plain chocolate or chocolate flake or
  chocolate vermicelli

Separate the eggs and put the whites in a clean, dry bowl.
  Beat the egg yolks with the honey.
  Chop the marshmallows.
  Blend the cornflour with some of the milk and put the rest
in a pan to heat. Pour over the mixed cornflour, return to the
pan and cook for 8–10 mins. slowly, stirring continuously.
Stir in the marshmallows over low heat until they are melted.
Remove from the stove and stir in the honey and fruit juices.
Leave in a cool place, stirring occasionally.
  When cold, whisk the egg whites until they are stiff. Fold
them into the mixture. Spoon into individual glasses and
decorate the tops with chocolate.

Cakes and Biscuits

PLAIN HONEY BISCUITS

50 g (2 oz) margarine
100 g (4 oz) plain flour
50 g (2 oz) castor or soft brown sugar
a pinch of salt
10 ml (1 dessertsp) honey

Cream the margarine, sugar and honey well together, sieve the
flour and salt and work into the creamed mixture. Knead until
smooth. Roll out to 6 mm ($\frac{1}{4}$ in) on a floured board and cut
into rounds. Prick with a fork and place on a baking sheet.
Bake for about 10 mins. at 350° F. Allow to cool a little before
removing from the tin.

   These biscuits will keep well for several weeks in an
airtight container.

HONEY GINGER BISCUITS

50 g (2 oz) margarine
40 g (1½ oz) castor sugar
30 ml (3 level dessertsps) honey
100 g (4 oz) plain flour
5 ml (1 level tsp) ground ginger
25 g (1 oz) rolled oats
2.5 ml (½ level tsp) bicarbonate of soda
10 ml (1 dessertsp) milk

Cream the margarine, sugar and honey until light and fluffy.
    Add flour, ginger, rolled oats and bicarbonate of soda
dissolved in milk, and mix well.
    Shape into small balls and put onto a greased baking sheet,
press each one with a fork to flatten it and mark the top.
    Bake for 15 to 20 mins. at 325° F until golden brown. Allow
to cool on a wire rack.

HONEY AND LEMON BISCUITS

75 g (3 oz) margarine
125 g (5 oz) flour
25 g (1 oz) soft brown sugar
40 ml (2 level tbs) honey
20 ml (1 tbs) lemon juice

Beat the margarine, sugar and honey until creamy.
    Work in the flour and lemon juice.
    Form into small balls with damp hands and put on a greased
baking sheet. Press with a fork to flatten.
    Bake for about 15 mins. at 350° F until golden brown.

OATMEAL BISCUITS—very good with cheese or marmite

100 g (4 oz) wholewheat flour
100 g (4 oz) fine oatmeal (coarse oatmeal can be
    ground in a coffee grinder)
5 ml (1 tsp) honey
75 g (3 oz) margarine
2.5 ml (½ tsp) vinegar
2.5 ml (½ tsp) bicarbonate of soda
a pinch of salt
a little milk

Rub the margarine into the flour and salt. Mix in the oatmeal.
    Dissolve the bicarbonate of soda in a little milk, stir in the
honey and vinegar and pour into the dry ingredients.
    Mix with the hands until it sticks together and will roll out.
    Roll on a floured board and cut into thin rounds.
    Put on a greased baking sheet and bake for about 15 mins.
at 350° F until firm and lightly brown.

DATE SHORTIES

150 g (6 oz) margarine
75 g (3 oz) castor sugar
150 g (6 oz) self-raising flour
150 g (6 oz) semolina
150 g (6 oz) dates
20 ml (1 tbs) honey
125 ml (¼ pint) water
10 ml (2 tsp) lemon juice or orange juice

Melt the margarine and sugar. Stir in the flour and semolina.
Add the sugar and stir.
    Spread half this mixture in a small swiss roll tin. Chop the
dates and put in a small saucepan with the honey, fruit juice
and water. Stir over gentle heat until thick and smooth.
    Spread this over the mixture in the tin.
    Cover with the rest of the pastry mixture.
    Smooth the top and bake at 350° F for 30–35 mins.
    When cool cut into fingers.

HONEY SANDWICH

150 g (6 oz) butter or margarine
100 g (4 oz) castor sugar
20 ml (1 tbs) honey
150 g (6 oz) self-raising flour
3 eggs
about 40 ml (2 tbs) warm water

Cream the margarine with the honey and sugar until light and fluffy. Gradually add the beaten eggs and mix in well.

Carefully fold in the sifted flour and add a little water, if required, to make a soft mixture.

Grease and line two 17.5 cm (7 in) sandwich tins.

Divide the mixture between the two tins and smooth over the tops.

Bake in the centre of a moderate oven, 350° F until golden and springy to the touch.

Cool on a wire rack.

HONEY BUTTER FILLING

50 g (2 oz) butter or margarine
75 g (3 oz) icing sugar
20 ml (1 tbs) honey

Cream the butter, beat in the sifted icing sugar until smooth then beat in the honey.

When the cake is cold sandwich together with the filling and dredge the top with icing sugar.

SCONES

200 g (8 oz) self-raising flour
65 g (2½ oz) margarine
a pinch of salt
10 ml (1 dessertsp) honey
5 ml (level tsp) golden raising powder
40 g (1½ oz) sultanas (optional)
125 ml (bare ¼ pint) sour milk

Rub the fat into the flour, salt and golden raising powder. Mix the honey with the milk, and add, with the sultanas, to the flour and mix to a soft dough.

Roll out to 1.5 cm (½ in) thick, cut into rounds or squares and place close together on a floured baking sheet. Brush the tops with milk. Place in an oven pre-heated to 425° F and cook at 400° F until well risen and golden brown on top.

PLUM COBBLER

Victoria plums
scone mixture (as above)
sugar

Cut the plums in half and remove the stones. Place in a pie dish and sprinkle with sugar to taste.

Cut circles of scone mixture and place on top of the plums to cover them. Bake at 400° F until the scone topping begins to brown. Lower the heat and continue cooking until the plums are soft.

Serve hot or cold.

DATE, HONEY AND WALNUT CAKE

200 g (8 oz) self-raising flour
125 g (5 oz) margarine
2 eggs
75 g (3 oz) castor sugar
75 g (3 oz) chopped dates
50 g (2 oz) chopped walnuts
50 g (2 oz) honey

Cream together the margarine, sugar and honey. Beat the eggs
and add to the creamed mixture. Sieve the flour and add with
the dates and walnuts. Mix well.

Pour into a greased and lined cake tin and bake at 325° F
for 1–1½ hours. Cool on a wire rack.

HONEY FRUIT CAKES

This is a rich mixture with a spongey texture. It will keep for
up to four weeks in an airtight tin and will freeze well. The
recipe given will make two 15 cm (6 in) cakes.

200 g (8 oz) margarine
125 g (5 oz) soft light brown sugar
100 g (4 oz) honey
3 eggs

300 g (12 oz) self-raising flour
80 ml (4 tbs) milk (approx)
300 g (12 oz) mixed dried fruit
grated rind of half a lemon or orange
flaked almonds to decorate top

Put the honey, sugar and half the milk in a basin and stand in a warm place until it has melted and the sugar dissolved. Allow to cool before using.

Cream the margarine, add the sugar and honey mixture and beat well.

Beat the eggs and add them gradually, beating well. Fold in the fruit and the sifted flour. The mixture should be a soft dropping consistency, add more milk as required.

Place the mixture in two greased and lined tins, sprinkle a few almonds on top and bake at 275° F for 1¼ hours. Allow to cool for about 10 mins. then carefully turn onto a wire rack to cool.

The following recipe is a semi-rich cake that also freezes well.

150 g (6 oz) margarine
125 g (5 oz) soft brown sugar
50 g (2 oz) honey
300 g (12 oz) self-raising flour
3 eggs
a little milk
grated rind of an orange
a little grated nutmeg
400 g (1 lb) mixed dried fruit

Cream the margarine with the honey and sifted sugar. Beat in the beaten eggs and grated rind.

Add the sifted flour, nutmeg and fruit. Mix with sufficient milk to make it a soft consistency.

Bake in two 15 cm (6 in) greased and lined tins at 300° F for 1¼–1½ hours.

Leave in the tin for 10 mins. and cool on a wire rack.

This recipe is for a plainer cake, very suitable for inclusion in a packed lunch etc. It will keep well for up to two weeks.

200 g (8 oz) self-raising flour
100 g (4 oz) butter or margarine
75 g (3 oz) soft brown or castor sugar
25 ml (1 tbs) honey
225 g (9 oz) mixed dried fruit
5 ml (1 tsp) grated orange rind
1 large egg
100 ml ($\frac{3}{4}$ gill) milk or milk and water mixed

Sift the flour, rub in the margarine lightly and add the remaining dry ingredients.

Lightly beat the egg and mix with the milk and honey. Add to the dry ingredients and mix well.

Bake in a lined and greased 17.5 (7 in) tin for about 1$\frac{1}{4}$ hours at 325° F.

A CONVENTIONAL HONEY CAKE

100 g (4 oz) margarine or butter
150 g (6 oz) honey
150 g (6 oz) sultanas
200 g (8 oz) self-raising flour
2 eggs
a pinch of salt
a little milk

Cream the fat and the honey, add the beaten eggs alternately with the flour and salt. Mix well. Add the sultanas and a little milk if needed.

Bake in a greased and lined 17.5 (7 in) tin for 1$\frac{1}{4}$–1$\frac{1}{2}$ hours at 325° F. If the edges appear to be cooking more than the middle lower the heat a little.

BANANA HONEY TEABREAD

175 g (7 oz) wholemeal flour
10 ml (2 tsps) baking powder
100 g (4 oz) soft brown sugar
50 g (2 oz) margarine

2 good sized bananas
50 g (2 oz) honey
1 egg
125 ml (¼ pint) milk

Put the sugar, margarine and eggs in a bowl and beat together until creamy. Beat in the bananas, mashed with the honey.

Sift the salt, flour, and baking powder into the bowl and beat in with the milk to make a soft, dropping consistency.

Pour into a well greased loaf tin and bake at 325–350° F for 1–1¼ hours, until it is firm in the middle.

Serve sliced with butter or margarine.

HONEY DATE AND WALNUT LOAF

200 g (8 oz) dates
40 g (1½ oz) chopped walnuts
125 ml (¼ pint) cold tea
50 g (2 oz) brown sugar
40 ml (2 tbs) honey
40 ml (2 tbs) water
1 egg
200 g (8 oz) self-raising flour
honey to glaze

Put the chopped dates in a bowl, mix the tea, honey, sugar and water together and pour over the dates. Leave to soak overnight or for about 8 hours.

Stir the mixture well and add the beaten egg. Stir in the sieved flour and chopped walnuts and stir until well mixed.

Put in a well greased loaf tin and bake for 1–1¼ hours at 325° F or until firm and brown.

Remove from the oven and brush the top with honey to make a glaze. Leave in the tin for 10 minutes, then cool on a wire rack.

Serve the loaf sliced and spread with butter or margarine.

This loaf will keep up to four weeks in an airtight tin.

HONEY FRUIT LOAF

Follow the above recipe using 200 g (8 oz) of mixed fruit instead of dates and walnuts.

HONEY AND ORANGE CAKE

100 g (4 oz) margarine
70 g (2½ oz) castor or soft brown sugar
50 g (2 oz) honey
150 g (6 oz) self-raising flour
20–40 ml (1–2 tbs) milk
2 eggs
grated rind of an orange
25 g (1 oz) candied peel
flaked almonds for decoration (optional)

Melt the honey, sugar and grated rind with the milk. Allow to cool before using.

Cream the margarine, add the sugar and honey mixture and beat in well. Add the eggs, well beaten a little at a time. Fold in the flour and candied peel. The mixture should be of a soft dropping consistency, add a little more milk if required.

Place the mixture in a greased and lined 17.5 cm (7 in) tin, sprinkle a few flaked almonds on top and bake for 1¼–1½ hours at 275–300° F until golden brown and firm.

Allow to cool for 10 mins. then turn carefully onto a wire rack.

HONEY AND LEMON CAKE

Follow the previous recipe using lemon rind instead of orange.

CHERRY TOPPED SQUARES

Topping
50 g (2 oz) glace cherries
75 g (3 oz) rolled oats
75 g (3 oz) desiccated coconut
50 g (2 oz) demerara sugar
75 g (3 oz) margarine
40 ml (2 tbs) honey

Cake
100 g (4 oz) butter or margarine
100 g (4 oz) castor sugar
2 eggs
100 g (4 oz) self-raising flour

36

Topping

Put the margarine and honey in a warm place until liquid.
Chop the cherries and put in a bowl with the oats, demerara
sugar and coconut and mix well. Add the melted margarine and
honey and stir until well blended.

Cake

Cream the margarine and sugar until light and fluffy, add the
beaten eggs and mix in well. Fold in the sifted flour to make a
soft dropping consistency. Add a little water if it appears too
stiff. Grease and line a 20 cm (8 in) square tin and spread out
smoothly. Spread the topping over it and bake for about
45–50 mins. at 350° F in the centre of the oven.

When done the top of the cake should spring back when
pressed with a finger. Allow it to cool in the tin before cutting
into squares.

COFFEE CRACKLES

These can be made in a few minutes and require no baking.

25 g (1 oz) margarine or butter
20 ml (1 tbs) honey
40 ml (2 tbs) liquid coffee essence
100 g (4 oz) sieved icing sugar
50 g (2 oz) cornflakes or rice crispies

Melt the margarine and honey in a pan gently.

Remove from the heat and add the coffee essence and icing
sugar. Stir in the cornflakes or rice crispies.

Spoon into paper cases and leave to set.

CHOCOLATE CRACKLES

Substitute 50 g (2 oz) of block chocolate for the coffee essence.
Melt it in a basin over hot water. Add the melted honey and
margarine as before and stir in the cornflakes or rice crispies.

HONEY CHEESECAKE

Pastry
175 g (7 oz) flour
a pinch of salt
100 g (4 oz) margarine
25 g (1 oz) castor or icing sugar
1 egg yolk
water

Sift the flour and salt into a bowl and rub in the fat. Add the sifted sugar and bind with an egg yolk and water.

Roll out the pastry to line an 18 cm (7 in) flan ring on a lightly greased baking sheet.

Bake blind for about 20 mins. at 375–400° F until set.

Filling
60 ml (3 tbs) honey
2 eggs
2.5 ml ($\frac{1}{2}$ tsp) ground nutmeg
175 g (7 oz) cream cheese
25 g (1 oz) chopped walnuts

Beat the cream cheese and honey until smooth. Add the beaten eggs and nutmeg and mix well. Pour the mixture into the flan case and bake at 350° F for 20 mins. Sprinkle the chopped nuts on top and cook for another 10 minutes until set.

Serve cold.

Honey in the Christmas Cooking

MINCEMEAT

Mincemeat made with some honey keeps well with an
improvement in flavour.

300 g (12 oz) seedless raisins
200 g (8 oz) candied peel
200 g (8 oz) sultanas
200 g (8 oz) currants
400 g (1 lb) apples
200 g (8 oz) margarine or suet
250 g (10 oz) brown sugar
grated rind and juice of 1 orange
grated rind and juice of 1 lemon
15 g ($\frac{1}{2}$ oz) mixed spice
50 g (2 oz) honey
brandy or rum (optional)

Mince the fruit, mix all ingredients together except the brandy.
Put all into a preserving pan, or any large pan that will fit into
the oven. Set the heat at 200° F and leave the pan in the oven
for about 8 hours, stirring every hour. It should never come
to the boil.

Remove from the oven and when cool add the brandy.

Pack into jars, pressing out any air bubbles and seal.

This should keep well for a year.

CHRISTMAS CAKE
(to fit a 17.5 cm (7 in) round tin)

300 g (12 oz) currants ⎤
125 g (5 oz) sultanas ⎬ washed and dried the
125 g (5 oz) stoned raisins ⎦ previous day
75 g (3 oz) cherries
50 g (2 oz) mixed candied peel
50 g (2 oz) sweet almonds
a little grated lemon rind
200 g (8 oz) plain flour
2.5 ml (½ tsp) ground cinnamon
2.5 ml (½ tsp) ground mace
150 g (6 oz) butter or margarine
100 g (4 oz) soft brown sugar
50 g (2 oz) honey
3 large eggs or 4 small eggs
(approximate weight when cooked 1.5 kilos [3¼ lb])

Prepare tin, grease and double line with greaseproof paper.
Chop the raisins, peel the almonds and quarter the cherries.
Sift the flour and spices and add the lemon rind.
Cream together the butter, sugar and honey until light and
fluffy. Add the beaten eggs gradually with a little flour. Fold
in the rest of the flour with the fruit and mix well. Turn into
the prepared tin, press down and hollow out the centre. Tie 4
thicknesses of brown paper round the outside of the tin and
stand it on a pad of paper in the centre of the oven. This will
avoid the outside being cooked more than the middle.
(Newspaper could be used and if it browns it is an indication
that the oven is too hot.)
Cook at 300° F for 2 hours then reduce the heat to 275° F
for another 1–1½ hours.
Cool for a time in the tin before turning out.
When cold, paint over it with a pastry brush dipped in
brandy. If the cake is baked well ahead this can be repeated at
weekly intervals.
When quite cold, wrap the cake in greaseproof paper, then in
foil and store in a cool place for 2–3 months.
Before applying the almond paste brush the cake over with
honey instead of the conventional jam. It will stick well.

Cooking with Yeast—Bread and Buns

When honey is used in place of sugar in breadmaking the result is a loaf which is slightly more moist with a good flavour.

Use your favourite recipe, using honey instead of sugar, but using just slightly more to allow for the extra liquid in the honey.

Note : When using English Wholewheat flour which has a low gluten content, either an egg or more yeast should be used to make it rise well.

If your hands are dipped in warm water before kneading dough it will not stick to them.

Bread dough does not stick to a plastic bowl and is easier to mix than in a china one.

WHOLEMEAL BREAD

1.5 kg (3 lb) wholemeal bread flour (or
    2 parts wholemeal and 1 part white flour)
20 ml (1 tbs) salt
25 g (1 oz) lard or margarine
25 g (1 oz) fresh yeast or 20 ml (1 tbs) dried yeast
15 ml (3 tsp) honey
1 litre (1½ pints) warm water
poppy seeds (optional)

41

Mix the flour and salt and rub in the fat.

Cream fresh yeast with some of the water and honey until liquid *or* take some of the water in a basin, add the honey and sprinkle the dried yeast on top. Leave in a warm place for 10–15 mins., then stir well with a fork.

Add the yeast and the remaining water to the flour and mix well with the hands. Turn onto a board or table and knead well for about 10 mins., when it should feel elastic.

Place the dough back in the bowl, cover with a piece of oiled plastic or a damp cloth and leave in a warm place until it has doubled in size.

Turn out of the bowl and knead for a few minutes.

Cut into 4 or 5 pieces and put into greased loaf tins, press the dough down and half fill each tin.

Paint the tops of the loaves with milk and sprinkle on poppy seeds.

Bake in an oven preheated to 450° F. After 5 mins. turn down to 400° F and cook for another 25 mins., until they are brown and sound hollow when tapped on the base.

Cool on a wire rack

QUICK WHOLEMEAL BREAD

1.5 kg (3 lb) stoneground wholewheat flour
20 ml (1 tbs) salt
40 g (2 oz or 1½ tbs) fresh yeast or 30 ml (1½ tbs) dried
    yeast
50 g (2 oz) butter, margarine or lard
30 ml (1½ tbs) honey
1 litre (1½ pints) warm water

Mix the flour and salt in a large bowl.
    Dissolve the honey in a little water, either sprinkle on the
dried yeast or cream in the fresh yeast.
    Warm the fat until it is melted but not hot.
    Make a well in the centre of the flour and add the yeast,
honey, fat and most of the water and mix it lightly and
thoroughly with the fingers.
    Add more water until the dough binds together and is
sticky but not wet.
    Knead well in the bowl or on a table top or board for about
10 to 20 minutes. By then it should feel like putty. Cut the
dough in pieces and press into well greased bread tins, to half
fill each tin.
    Cover with oiled polythene or a damp cloth and leave in a
warm place for about 40 minutes or until they have doubled
in size.
    Put in an oven preheated to 450° F and lower the heat to
400° F after 15 minutes. Cook for another 15 minutes or until
they look cooked and sound hollow when tapped.

WHOLEMEAL BREAD ROLLS

Use either of the two recipes for wholemeal bread. Instead of
putting the loaves into tins, cut the dough into small pieces,
about half the size of a cooked roll, put the pieces after rounding
in the hands, onto a greased baking sheet and allow to double
in size. Bake at 450° F for about 10 mins.

WHITE BREAD

1.5 kg (3 lb) strong white bread flour
25 ml (1 tbs) salt
25 g (1 oz) lard or margarine
25 g (1 oz) fresh yeast or 25 ml (1 tbs) dried yeast
10 ml (1 dessertsp) honey
1 litre (1½ pints) warm water

Mix flour and salt, rub in the fat.

Cream fresh yeast with a little water and honey *or* stir the honey into about 150 ml (5 fl. oz) of water and sprinkle the dried yeast on top. Leave for 10 mins. then mix in with a fork.

Add the yeast and the remaining water to the flour mixture. Mix well, then turn onto a board or table and knead well for about 10 minutes.

Place the dough in a greased bowl, cover with a piece of oiled polythene or a damp cloth, and leave in a warm place for about an hour, until it has doubled in size.

Turn dough out and knead for another 5 minutes. Grease loaf tins. Divide into pieces and press into tins to half fill them.

Brush tops with milk or water and leave until doubled in size.

Bake in a preheated oven at 450° F for 10 minutes and then reduce heat to 400° F for a further 20 minutes.

The loaves should be golden brown and sound hollow when tapped. If a more crusty loaf is required, remove from the tins and return to the oven for a few minutes.

WHITE BREAD ROLLS

Follow the previous recipe, but instead of putting the dough into bread tins, roll it into balls and put on a greased baking sheet. Allow to rise then bake at 450° F for about 10 minutes. Poppy seeds can be sprinkled on top before cooking if liked.

Home made bread will keep fresh for a week and is excellent for deep freezing.

MILK BREAD

1.5 kg (3 tbs) strong plain flour
20 ml (1 tbs) salt
75 g (3 oz) margarine or butter
25 g (1 oz) yeast
1 litre (1½ pints) of milk or milk and water mixed
    (dried milk is quite satisfactory)
20 ml (1 tbs) honey

Put the milk (or milk and water) in a saucepan and heat to just
below boiling point. Remove from the heat and stir in the
butter or margarine until melted. Leave until lukewarm.

Cream fresh yeast with a little water and honey or sprinkle
dried yeast on top.

Sift the flour and salt into a large bowl and make a well in
the centre. Add the yeast, milk and honey and mix well until
it begins to come away from the sides of the bowl without
sticking. Turn onto a floured board or table top and knead for
about 10 mins. until the dough becomes elastic.

Return to the bowl, cover with greased polythene or a damp
cloth and leave in a warm place until it has doubled in size.

Turn out of the bowl and knead again for 4–5 min.

Cut into loaves and press into well greased loaf tins to half
fill them.

Glaze the tops with egg and milk, or milk and poppy seeds.

Put into a preheated oven and bake at 450° F for 10 mins.,
then lower heat and cook for a further 20–30 mins. at 425° F.
Remove from the oven and cool on a wire rack.

If a crusty loaf is required remove from the tins and replace
the loaves in the oven for a few minutes.

FRUIT LOAF

Use the previous recipe adding 300 g (12 oz) dried fruit at the
second kneading.

NUT LOAF

At the second kneading add 200–300 g (8–12 oz) chopped nuts,
walnuts, hazelnuts etc.

BAPS

1.5 kg (3 lb) plain flour
1 litre (1½ pints) milk and water or 1 litre (1½ pints)
  water and 50 g (2 oz) dried milk powder
150 g (6 oz) margarine
30 ml (1½ tbs) salt
25 g (1 oz) yeast
15 ml (3 tsp) honey

Put the milk and water into a saucepan and heat to just below boiling point. Remove from the heat and stir in the margarine until melted. Leave to cool to lukewarm.

Cream the yeast with the honey and a little warm water.

Sieve the flour and salt into a large bowl, make a well in the centre and add the yeast mixture and the cooled milk mixture.

Mix well, then turn out and knead for 10–20 mins. until the dough is smooth and elastic.

Return to the bowl, cover, and leave in a warm place until it has doubled in size.

Shape into about 24 baps. Put them on a floured baking tray and dust them with flour. Leave in a warm place until they have doubled in size.

Preheat the oven to 425° F and bake for 5 mins., reduce the heat to 400° F and bake for a further 10 mins.

FRUIT OR CURRANT BUNS

600 g (1½ lb) strong white flour
25 g (1 oz) fresh yeast
100 g (4 oz) margarine or butter
75 g (3 oz) sugar
20 ml (1 tbs) honey
a pinch of salt
250–275 ml (about ½ pint) warm milk
250 g (10 oz) currants or mixed fruit
40 ml (2 tbs) milk and 40 ml (2 tbs) honey for glaze

Sieve the sugar, salt and flour into a bowl. Warm the milk and
honey and melt the margarine. When lukewarm add these to
the flour with the creamed yeast. Knead thoroughly until
smooth and elastic, adding a little more water if required.
Return to the bowl and leave, covered, in a warm place until it
has doubled in size.

Knock the dough down and knead in the fruit. Shape into
buns and prove for 30–45 mins. until doubled in size.

Bake in a preheated oven for 5 minutes at 425° F and a
further 20 mins. at 400° F. Remove from the oven and brush
the tops while hot with a syrup made from milk and honey.

CURRANT BREAD OR FRUIT LOAF

Instead of shaping into buns put the dough into greased bread
tins and cook at 425° F for 10 mins. and 400° F for a further
20 mins. Glaze the tops as for buns.

HOT CROSS BUNS

5 ml (1 tsp) salt
400 g (1 lb) strong flour
25 g (1 oz) yeast
50 g (2 oz) margarine
40 g (1½ oz) moist or soft brown sugar
20 ml (1 tbs) mixed spice
1 egg
20 ml (1 tbs) honey
100 g (4 oz) currants
50 g (2 oz) candied peel
about 250 ml (½ pint) milk (warmed to blood heat)
(This quantity makes about 20 buns)

Sieve flour, salt and spice into a bowl.

Melt the margarine and honey, cream the yeast with a little milk.

Make a well in the centre of the flour and add the margarine, sugar, honey, milk, yeast and beaten egg.

Knead well, adding more milk if needed. (It should be a fairly stiff dough.) Add the fruit and knead it in.

Cover with polythene or a damp cloth and leave to rise for about 2 hours in a warm place or overnight in a cool place.

Knock down the dough and shape into buns. Set to prove for about half an hour.

Mark crosses with a paper knife or make them with pastry.

Bake in a hot oven, preheated to 425° F for 5 mins. Reduce heat and bake for a further 10 mins. at 400° F.

Glaze with honey syrup while still hot.

HOT CROSS BUNS OR SPICED BUNS (without eggs)

1 kilo (2 lb) strong flour
5 ml (1 tsp) salt
25 g (1 oz) yeast
500 ml (1 pint) milk and water
  (dried milk is good in this recipe)
30 ml (1½ tbs) mixed spice
100 g (4 oz) margarine
75 g (3 oz) soft dark brown sugar
20 ml (1 tbs) honey
200 g (8 oz) mixed fruit
50 g (2 oz) candied peel
Honey and milk to glaze (40 ml [2 tbs] of each)
(This quantity makes about 40 buns.)

The method is the same as for the previous recipe.

SPICY BUN LOAF

Follow the previous recipe, but cutting the dough into 3 or 4
pieces and putting them in greased bread tins. Cook for about
25–30 mins. and glaze the tops while hot.

Honey Spreads

HONEY BUTTER
100 g (4 oz) butter
30 ml (1½ tbs) honey
5 ml (1 tsp) lemon juice or orange juice

Blend the ingredients well together and use to spread on bread, toast and biscuits. This is a favourite with children and not so sticky for babies as when honey and butter are spread separately.

HONEY SOLDIERS
Blend approximately equal quantities of butter and honey.
    Spread on a slice of bread or toast and cut into strips.

HONEY AND NUT SPREAD
50 g (2 oz) butter or margarine
60 ml (3 level tbs) honey
50 g (2 oz) chopped nuts

Cream the margarine and honey, stir in the nuts. Serve in sandwiches, with wholemeal bread, or on oatmeal biscuits.

BANANA SPREAD
Mash a banana with honey and spread on bread for children.

Preserves

HONEY LEMON CHEESE
500 ml (1 pint) honey
4 eggs plus 2 yolks
the juice of 4 lemons
the finely grated rind of 2 lemons
75 g (3 oz) butter
(this recipe is best when a lightly flavoured honey is used)

Lightly beat the eggs and yolks.
    Put all the ingredients in the top of a double saucepan, or in a basin standing in a pan of heated water.
    Stir over low heat until the mixture thickens and will coat the back of a spoon.
    Pour into small warmed jars. Cover with waxed discs and cellophane jampot covers while hot.
    This preserve will keep for a long time.

BLACKCURRANT JELLY
Cook blackcurrants with just enough water to cover them until the juice is extracted, and the skins soft. Press fruit against the side of the pan occasionally to release the pectin from the skins. Strain through a jelly bag or muslin without squeezing.
    To each pint of juice allow 350 g (12 oz) of sugar. Dissolve the sugar then boil hard until it sets when tested. Remove from the heat, allow to cool a little, then stir in 200 g ($\frac{1}{2}$ lb) of honey for every pint of juice used.
    Pour into jars and seal.
    This is very soothing for colds and coughs. It can be used spread on bread or in drinks.

Beverages

BLACKCURRANT DRINK
5 ml (1 tsp) blackcurrant jelly
10 ml (2 tsp) honey
the juice of half a lemon (optional)

Put the fruit juice and jelly in a glass or mug and pour on hot water. Stir to dissolve and add the honey.

(On a cold night 10 ml [1 dessertsp] of rum added makes a very warming drink.)

HONEY LEMON TEA
For each glass allow:
10 ml (2 tsp) honey
250 ml (½ pint) hot weak tea
2 thin slices lemon

Place the honey in a heatproof glass, add the tea and stir to dissolve. Cut a lemon slice in half and put in the glass. Cut the second slice halfway across and place on the rim of the glass. Serve hot.

EGG WHIP
1 egg
250 ml (½ pint) water
1 peeled orange with pips removed
20 ml (1 tbs) honey

Blend all the ingredients together in a liquidizer. Pour into a glass to serve.

52

AN OLD FASHIONED COUGH REMEDY

1 lemon
40 ml (2 tbs) glycerine
100 g (4 oz) honey

Boil the lemon very slowly for 10 mins. This will soften it so
that more juice will come out. Cut it in half when cool and
squeeze out the juice.

Add the glycerine and honey and mix well together.

Pour into a bottle and use as required, taking a 5 ml
spoonful at a time. Always shake the bottle before using.

This mixture will not upset the stomach as many cough
medicines do.

If you need some cough remedy but do not have a lemon it
could be made with cider vinegar.

HONEY AT BEDTIME

For those who find it not easy to get off to sleep a bedtime
drink with honey is often helpful. Add a heaped 5 ml (1 tsp)
spoon of honey to a cup of warm milk and stir until it is
dissolved. If a fairly strong flavoured honey is used it will
make a very pleasant drink and sleep should come easily.

If you find milk not easily digested at night try a spoonful
of honey in hot water. If this seems too sweet add a few drops
of lemon juice.

A HONEY 'NIGHTCAP'

(This is particularly good for anyone with a cold.)

1 glass milk
10 ml (1 dessertsp) honey
10 ml (1 dessertsp) rum or whisky

Heat the milk but do not let it boil. Pour into a glass or mug
and stir in the honey. When dissolved stir in the rum or
whisky and drink at once.

HONEY HOT TODDY

This drink is suitable for a winter party.

1 bottle dry wine
1 lemon
3 cloves
1 stick of cinnamon
a small piece of mace
80 ml (4 tbs) brandy
150 g (6 oz) honey

Warm the wine, lemon rind, lemon juice and spices but do not boil. Remove from the heat, stir in the honey and leave with the lid tightly on for about an hour. Strain the liquid and reheat to drinking temperature, add the brandy and serve.

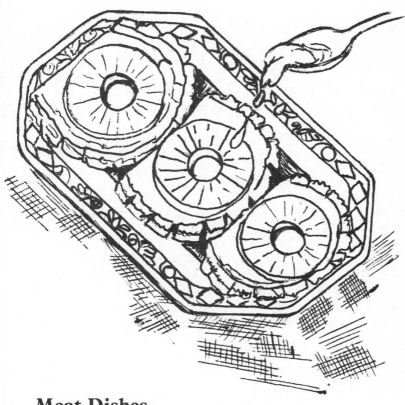

Meat Dishes

GAMMON SLICES WITH PINEAPPLE

slices of gammon
a pineapple ring for each slice (either tinned or fresh)
honey to glaze

Place the slices of gammon in a fireproof dish.

On each slice place a ring of pineapple.

Pour 1–5 ml (1 tsp) spoon of honey onto each ring of pineapple.

Cover with a lid or foil and cook in the oven for about 30 mins. at 350° F.

Apple rings could be used instead of pineapple.

SPICED GAMMON SLICES

This recipe is cooked on top of the stove and could be used when only a ring or picnic cooker is available.

gammon steaks or slices—1 per person
for each piece of gammon—4 whole cloves
                                    1–5 ml (1 tsp) mustard powder
                                    5 ml (1 tsp) honey
                                    1 slice of pineapple or apple
oil for frying

Heat the oil in a pan and fry the pineapple or apple rings for about 4 mins. Put in a warm place until the meat is done.

Stick the cloves in the steaks and fry them for about 5 mins. on one side.

Turn them and coat the cooked side with the mustard powder mixed to a paste with the honey. The back of a spoon can be used for this. Fry the second side until done, then serve hot with the apple or pineapple on top.

This can be served either with hot vegetables or a watercress salad.

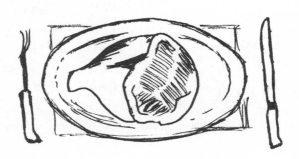

HAM WITH HONEY AND CIDER GLAZE

a ham or bacon joint—gammon, corner etc.
20 ml (1 tbs) honey
a pinch of powdered cloves
5 ml (1 tsp) mustard powder
125 ml (¼ pint) cider

Put the joint in a pan and cover with water. Bring to the boil and then pour off the water. Return the pan to the stove and add water to come about halfway up the joint. Simmer for 1–1½ hours according to size.

Drain off the water and cut the outer skin off the meat.

Score the fat in diamonds and spread the honey, mustard and cloves, mixed to a paste, over it.

Put the meat into a casserole and pour the cider over it. Bake for about 30 mins. at 400° F. Serve hot with pease pudding.

PEASE PUDDING

Soak 75 g (3 oz) split peas (green or yellow) overnight or for a few hours. Tie in a muslin bag and cook in the water with the bacon. Turn into a basin, add a knob of butter or margarine and beat to a cream. Serve hot with the meat.

ROAST CHICKEN

To cook a chicken with a slightly 'different' flavour, coat it before roasting with the following ingredients beaten to a cream.

25 g (1 oz) butter, margarine or cooking oil
20 ml (1 tbs) honey
2.5 ml (½ tsp) marjoram
seasoning to taste

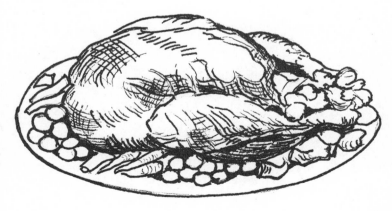

SWEET AND SOUR RED CABBAGE

1 small or half a large red cabbage
1 apple
1 medium sized onion
20 ml (1 tbs) honey
20 ml (1 tbs) vinegar (wine, cider or white vinegar)
cooking oil
salt and pepper

Chop the onion and apple and thinly slice the cabbage.

Put a little cooking oil in a saucepan and gently fry the onion and apple until they begin to look transparent. Add the honey, vinegar and cabbage slices.

Stir well, then add just enough water to prevent the mixture from sticking to the pan.

Lightly season, and simmer very gently with the lid on until cooked (about 15 to 20 mins.).

Stir at intervals and add a little more water if it becomes too dry.

Serve with pork dishes, chicken, ham, savoury pies etc.

Index of Recipes